AF326636

DEFINE

DEEP

Conversations
Kyna Teresa Teei

FIRST EDITION
DEFINE DEEP

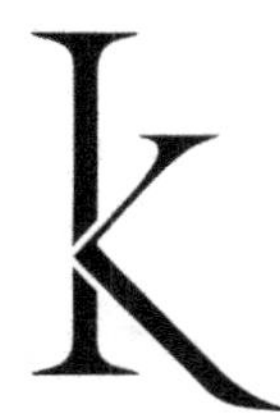

DEDICATED TO SOLUTIONS ...

ACKNOWLEDGEMENTS TO MY FAMILY, TRIBE, COMMUNITY, SUMA,
SONIA.T, LEONA.L, WAHIDA, LEV & ELIZABETH D, OLIVER.S,
GRANT.H, TAMIM.R, KATHRYN, ROSEMARY, CLINT, GAIL,
NAWEL.T, TABBY.H, BELLA, ROULA, MAHMOUD.T,
LAUREN, DEBBIE.O, BRIDGETTE, KAREN.C,
SILVANA, SIENNA, TIANA,

I WOULD LIKE TO HONOUR MY GRANDMOTHER RANGI
MY LOVING PARENTS, TITA, ROSEMARY
GRANDPARENTS TEEI, TEREAPII, ALEX
RAZIYE, ISA, ISAAK, KALEELA, TAMA
MARY, JASMINE, JUNIOR, DANIEL
NEPHEWS, NIECES
NATASHA.W
BROOKE

CHARLES.L
BUSYBIRD PUBLISHING

ACKNOWLEDGEMENT & HONOUR
WITH DEEPEST THANKS TO
JOHNNY.F

K.T

k

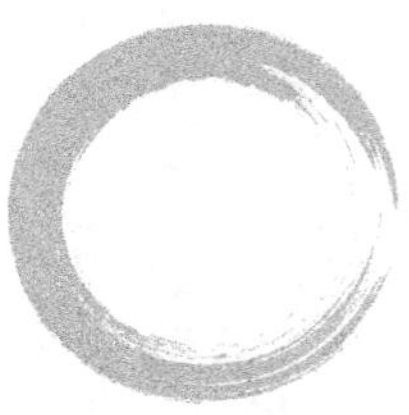

NATURALNESS
PROVOKED SINCERE STRUCTURES

k

WHEN DESIRES ARRIVE
FLAWS ARE NOT OFTEN SIGHTED

k

INTRODUCE CLARITY TO OUTSHINE RESISTANCE

k

BOLDNESS & CLARITY
MINIMISES
DOUBT

k

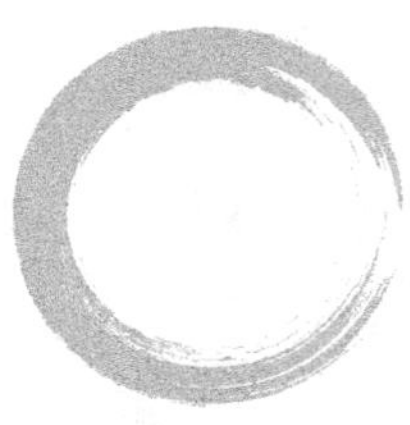

A CLEAR PLAN WILL TAKE YOU FURTHER
UNLIKE THE ONE YOU ARE
UNSURE OF

k

AS KNOWLEDGE DEEPENS
DESIRES MAY DISAPPEAR

K

ALL HAVE THEIR
STRENGTHS & WEAKNESSES

k

STEP BACK SOMETIMES, TO APPRECIATE
TO OBSERVE OR TO
WALK AWAY

k

CLEAR PLANS
PRODUCED PRACTICAL SOLUTIONS

k

EFFECTIVE PREVENTION ARRIVED FROM DEVELOPED EMOTIONAL RESPONSES

k

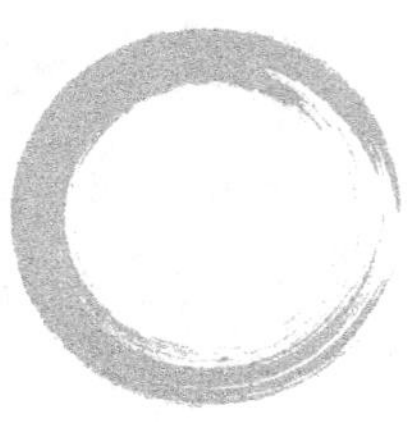

THE
PROFUSION IN ELEMENTS

k

REFINED
PREFERENCE OF PERCEPTION

K

THE VIBRATION WILL ADJUST
THE ESSENCE

k

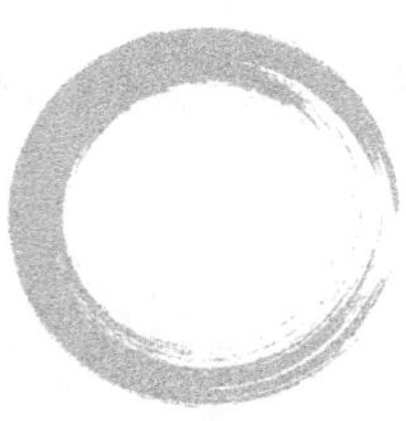

REFLECT ON THE EFFECT TO CREATE
A PRODUCTIVE
FLOW STATE

k

REFLECTING WHILE DESIGNING
ALLOWED RADIANCE
TO ARISE

k

THERE IS A NATURAL CAPACITY TO
NAVIGATE FROM SHATTERED
EXPECTATIONS

K

ALTERED CONCEPTS GENERATE
POWERFUL BREAKTHROUGHS

K

NOTED THE VALUES & MEANINGS
VIEWED ACCORDING TO THE
INDIVIDUALS PERSPECTIVE

k

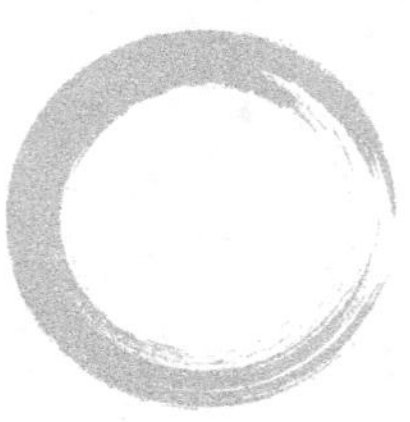

ALERT EYES
VIEWING SIMPLICITY

k

MAGNIFY
STRUCTURES & SETTLE SENSES

K

ABOVE THE SETBACKS
COURAGE & PERSISTENCE
WERE SELECTED

K

VIGILANT WITH CHOICES
OR
IMPULSIVE WITH DISTRACTIONS

k

A SENSE OF
IMPORTANCE & PURPOSE
COULD CLARIFY DECISIONS

k

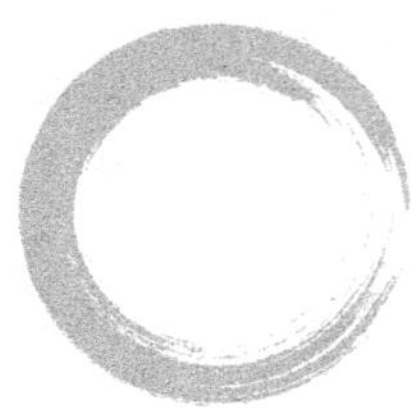

THE CONVERSATION CONNECTED
WITH SACRED TRUST & KNOWLEDGE
IGNITED TIME-HONOURED SOLUTIONS

k

PROGRESSING WITH INNOVATIVE CONSIDERATIONS IN MODERN SOCIETY

k

ADVANCE
WITH THE HONOURED & RESPECTED WHO INTEND NO HARM

k

PRODUCE
UNIQUE & VALUABLE
DESIGNS FROM PIVOTAL MOMENTS

K

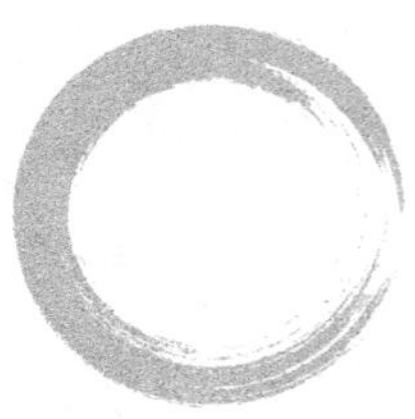

DEEP-ROOTED COURAGE
AFTER SHADOWS OF UNRESOLVED FEAR

k

CONSCIOUS WITH STRENGTH & ENERGY
ENABLES A STEADY PACE

k

AIMLESS
ILLUSIONS EXPIRED

k

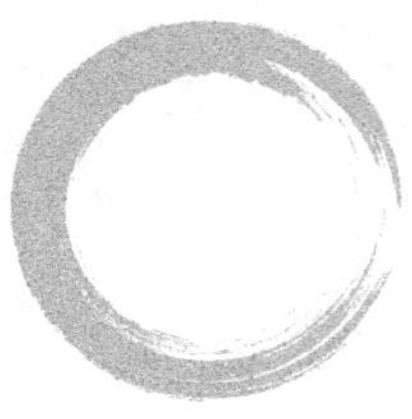

PERSEVERANCE
BEYOND THE DEFAULT

k

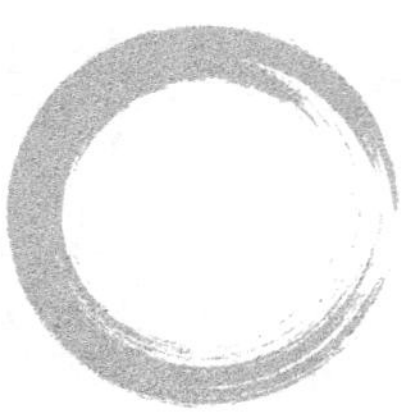

ACTIVE
ALIGNED & ALIVE

k

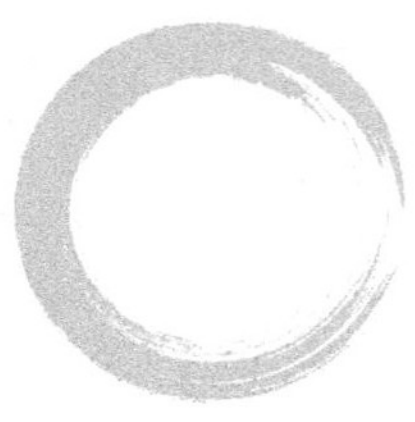

DISCIPLINE
DIMINISHED THE DESIRE

k

MIRRORLIKE
REFLECTIONS COULD
EXHIBIT VAGUE OR SUITABLE BONDS

k

CALM & RELAXED
WHILE ADDING SPICE ALLOWED
ELEVATION BEYOND NORMAL STANCES

k

THE STANCE OF THE CHARACTER
WITH HUMBLE REGARDS

K

INTRINSIC HARMONISED CONNECTIONS
ARE INDEED ANOTHER LEVEL

k

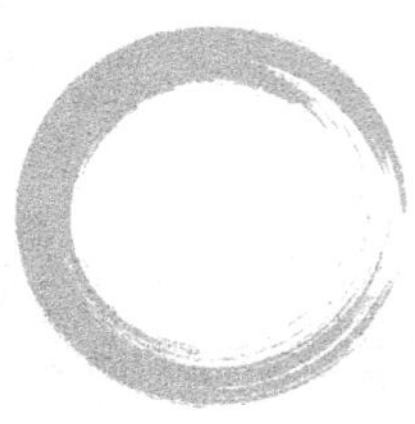

VALUED REFINED TECHNIQUES WHEN STRENGTHENING INTERNAL & EXTERNAL SUCCESS

k

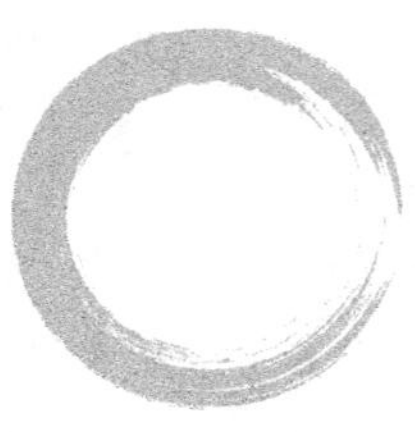

CAPTIVATED BY
THE FASCINATING STORIES

k

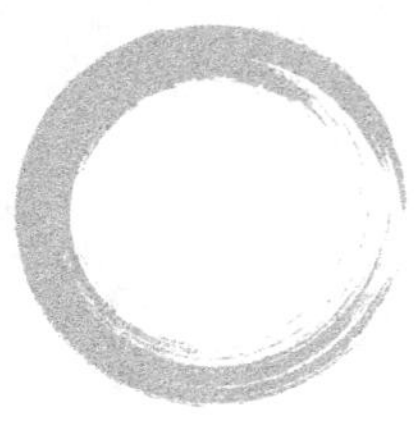

COMPATIBLE
OR NOT COMPATIBLE
INCREASED BLOOD PRESSURE COULD
DECREASE EFFECTIVE COMMUNICATION

K

QUITTING INADEQUATE INVESTMENTS WAS 'THE POWER MOVE'

k

SIGHT DIFFERENT ANGLES & LIGHT
TO ACKNOWLEDGE FACTORS
NOT OFTEN SEEN

k

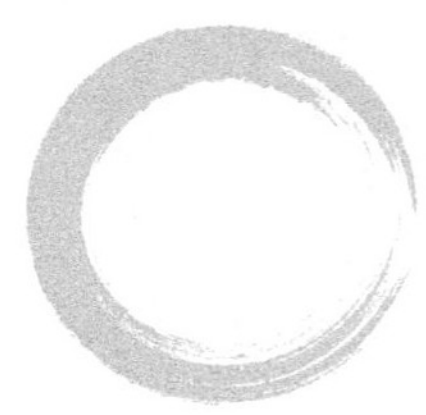

FINELY ALTERED REALITY ENCOURAGED
THOUGHTS VALUE TO BE EXCLUDED

K

FUTURE PROJECTS ATTRACT FRESH VENTURES CONNECTION IMPORTANCE INSIGHT SKILLS

K

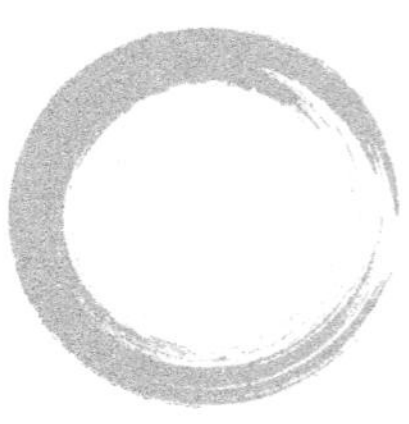

THE EQUATION PROMPTS WHERE ATTENTION & TIME IS REQUIRED FOR SOLUTIONS

k

THE CONVERSATION LEAD TO A
CULTIVATED SENSE OF WONDER

THE IDEAL TIME TO BE ATTENTIVE,
LISTEN, CONTRIBUTE & PERHAPS
DISCOVER ANOTHER
PERSPECTIVE

k

UNIVERSAL SKILLS
CREATED UNIVERSAL SOLUTIONS
GENERALISATION NOT SPECIALISATION

k

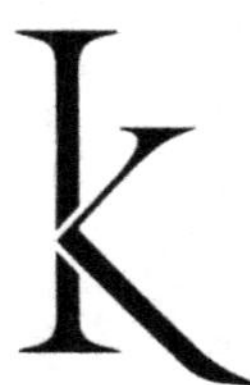

WISHING YOU THE BEST IN THIS JOURNEY OF LIFE

K.T